JH Fleming
colorblind
photography

Being colorblind gives an advantage when composing black & white… less confusion.
This special collection selected from thousands of captures. All images were framed
in the camera and presented without edits, genuine as seen through the lens.
Panchromatic conversion applied by unique proprietary process.
Original fine art and custom work available.

info@ BEACHNOISE.com

Joseph Fleming

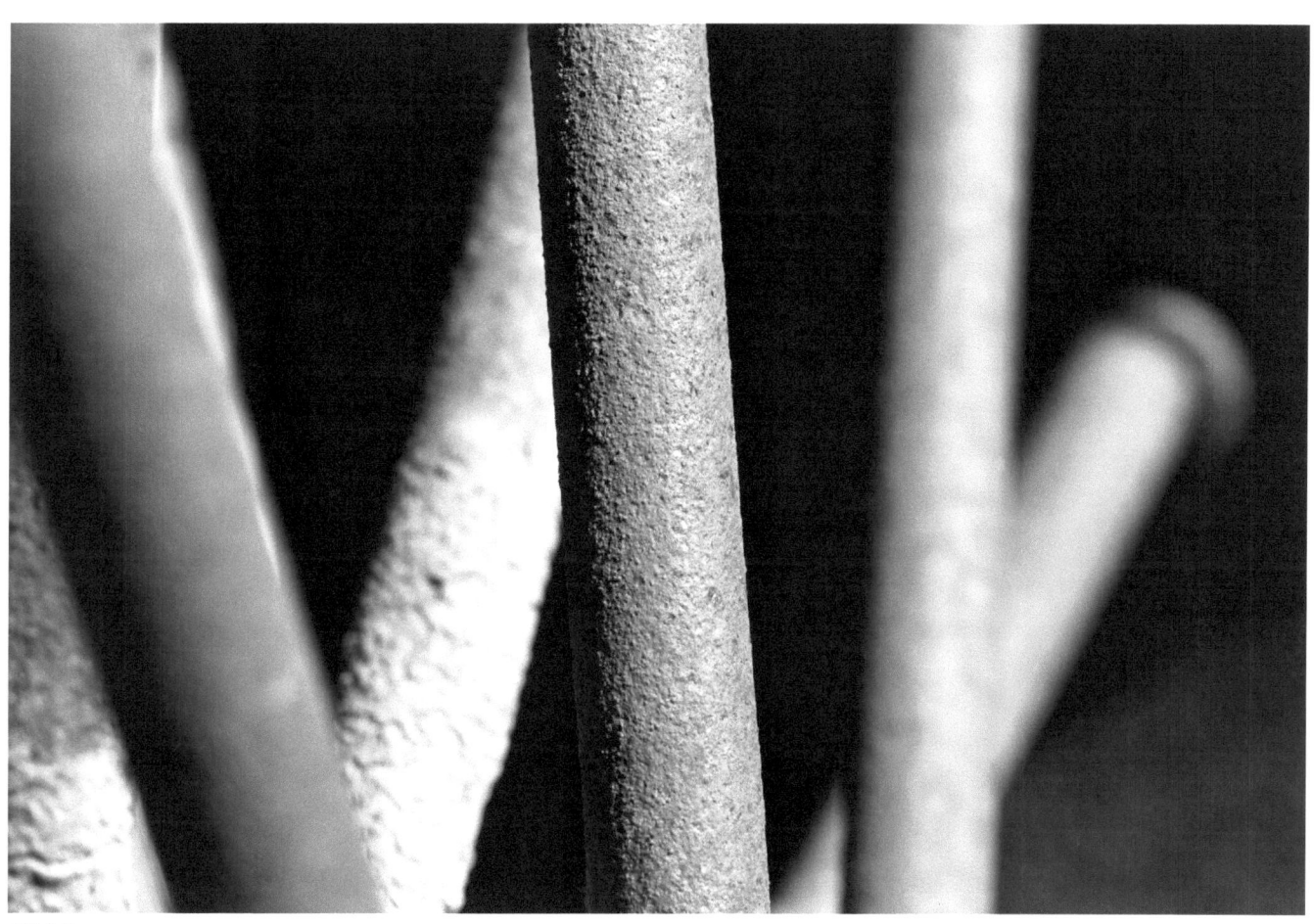

0780

1

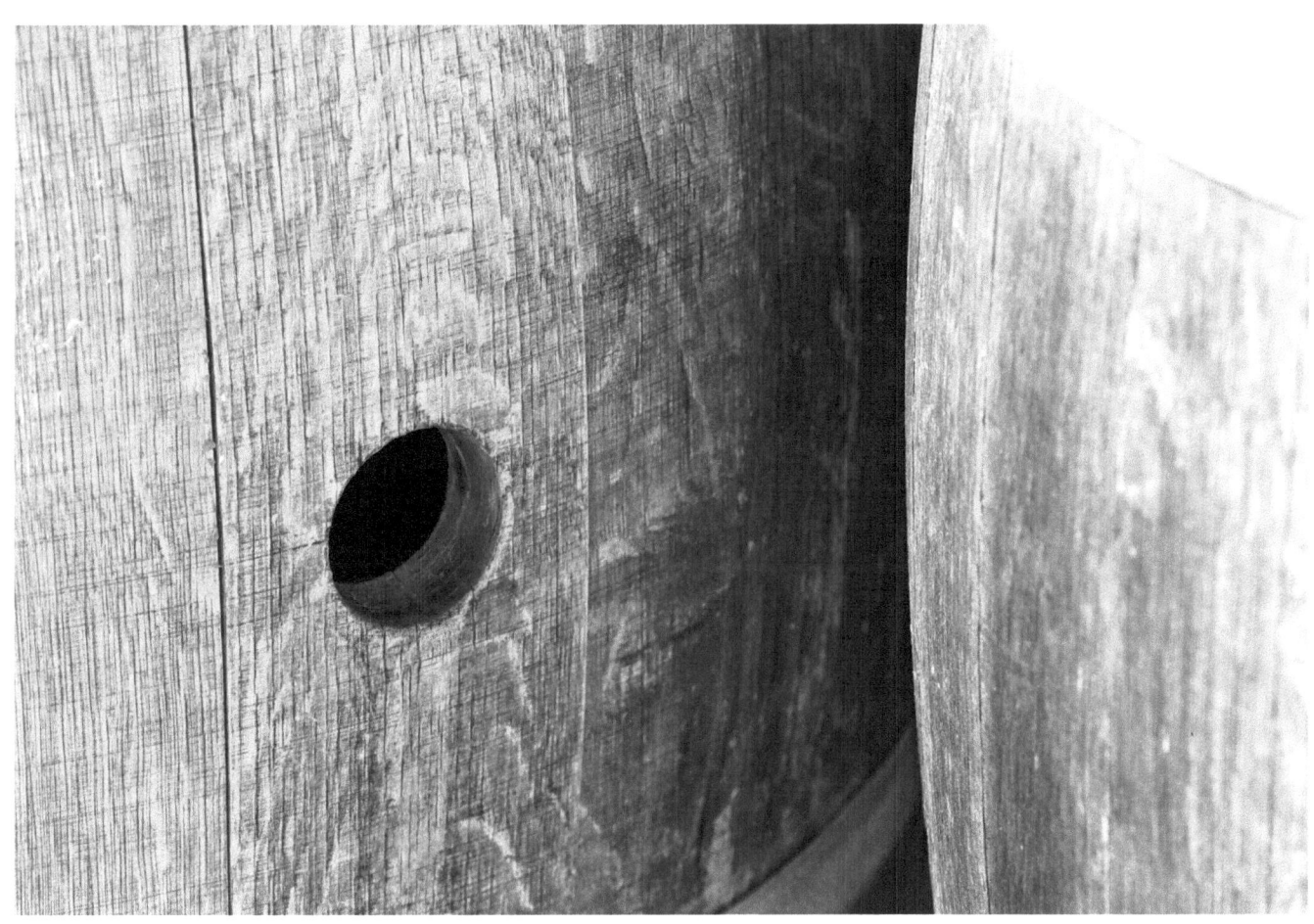

0826

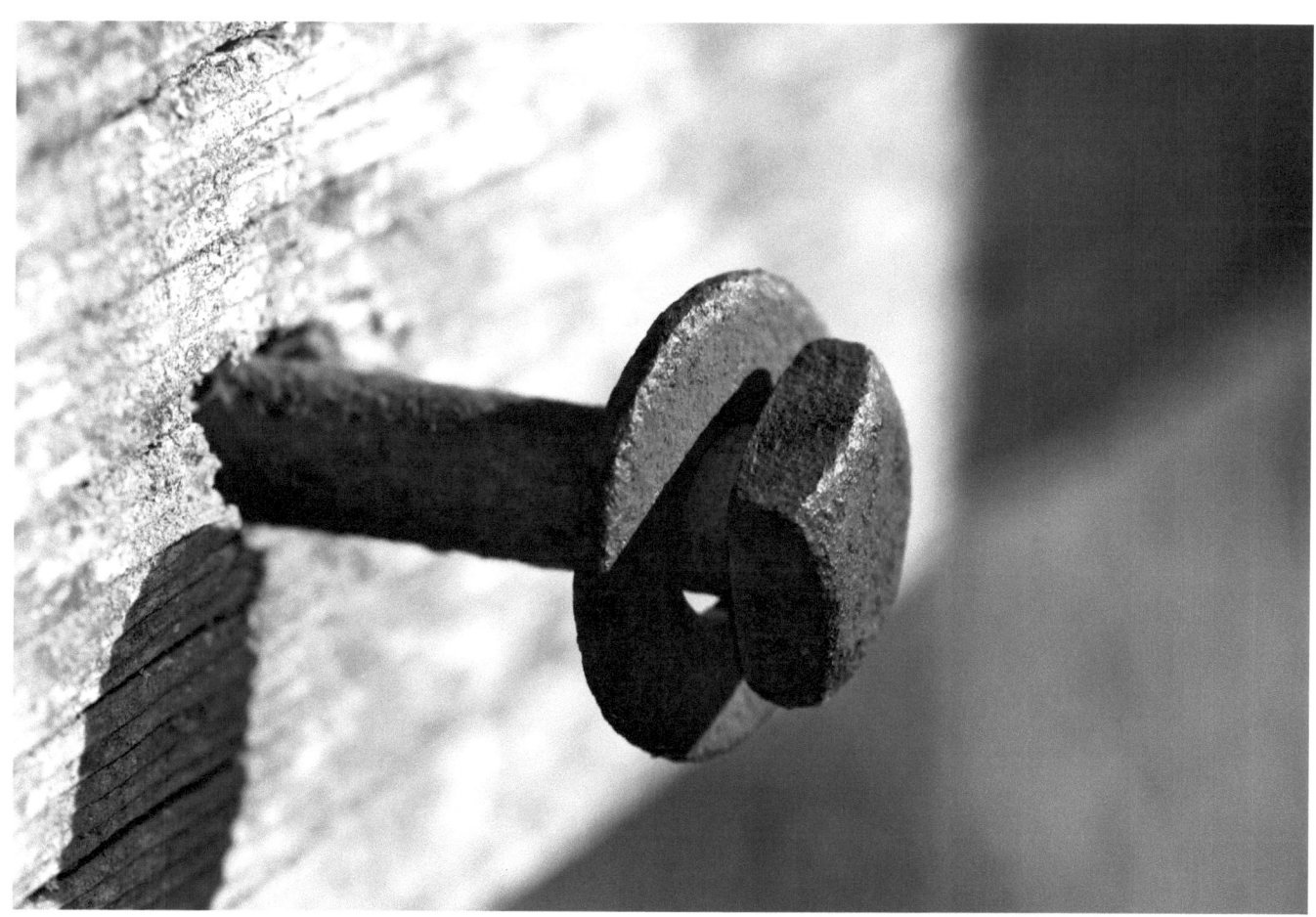

1173

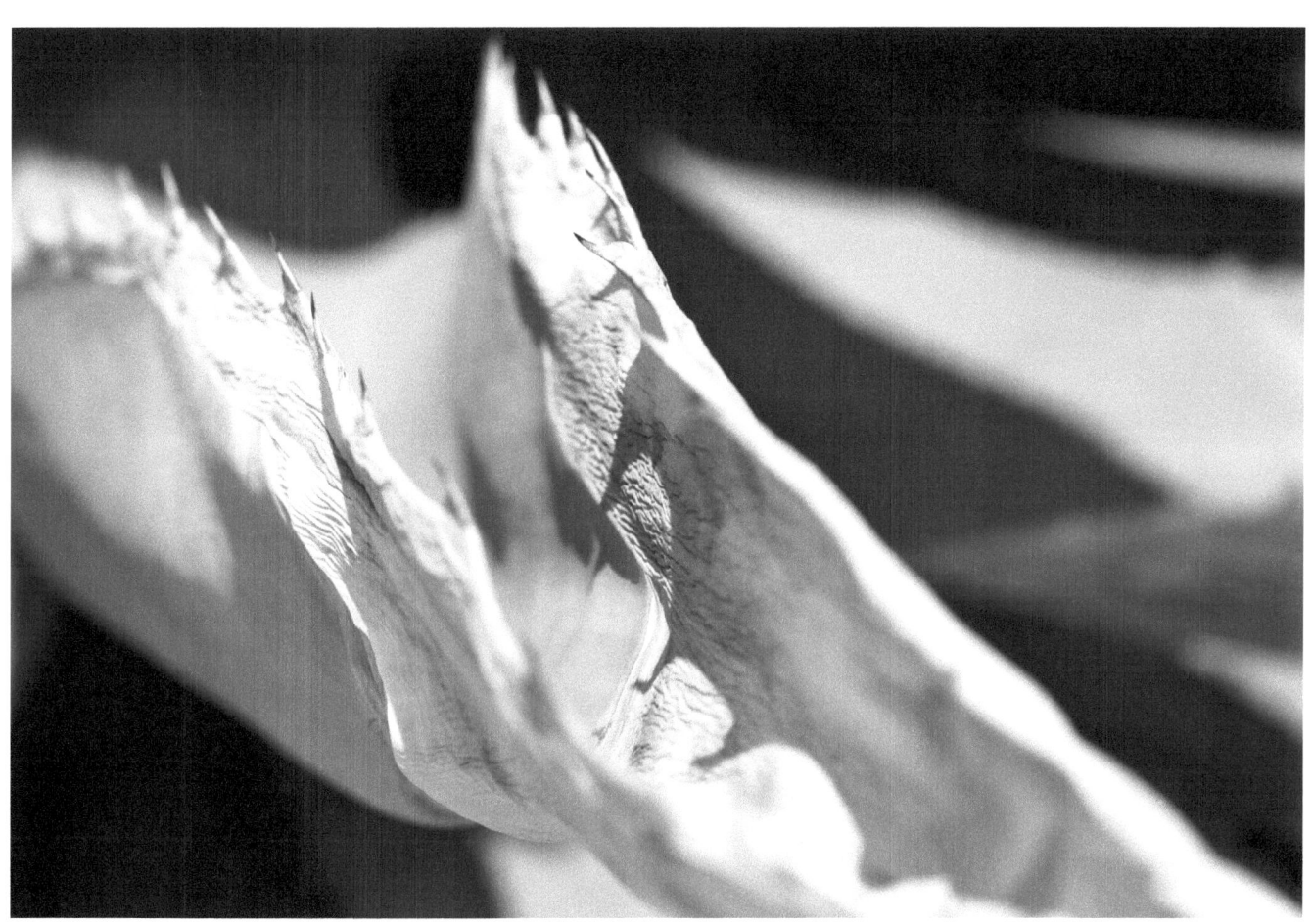

1581

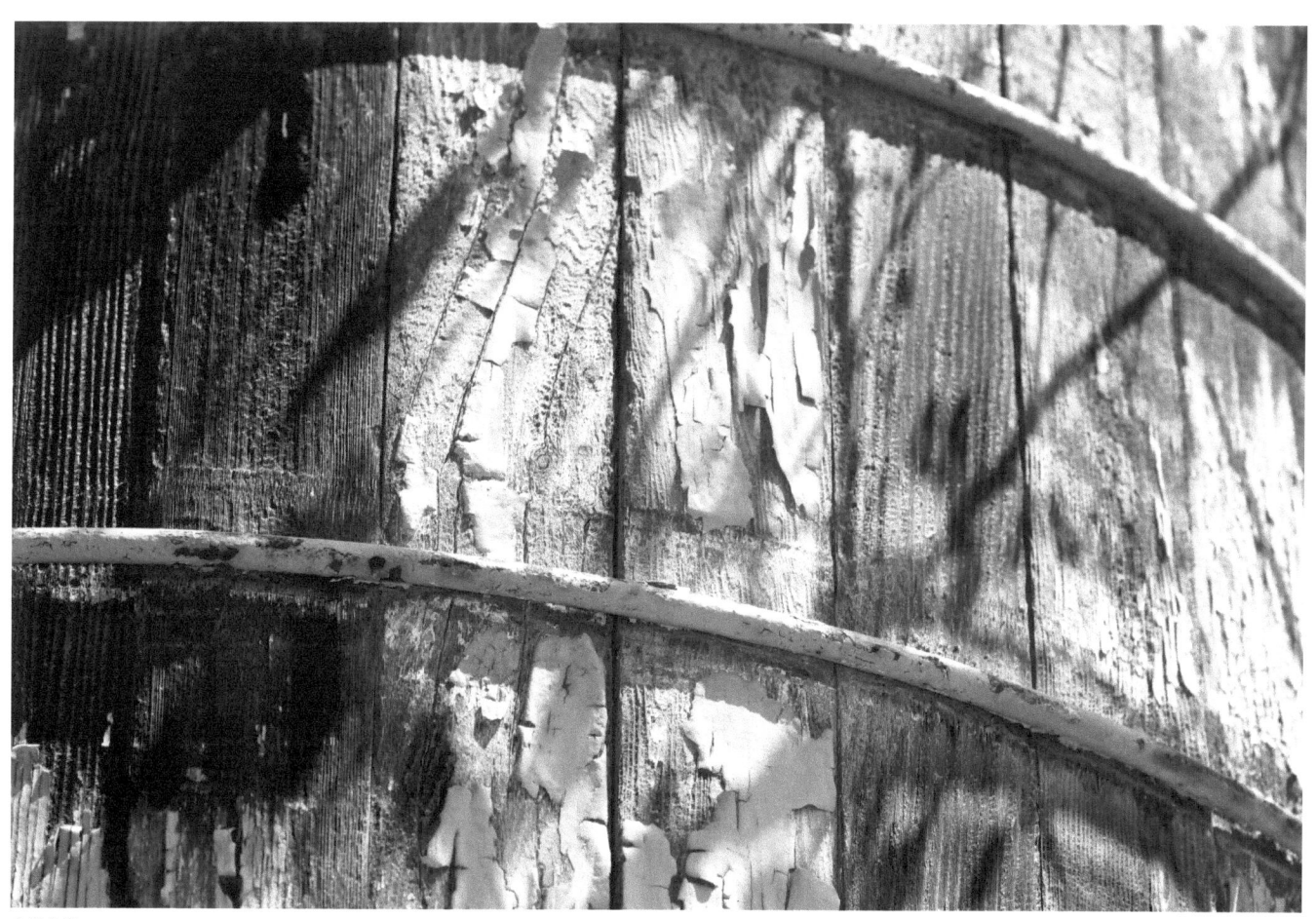

1608

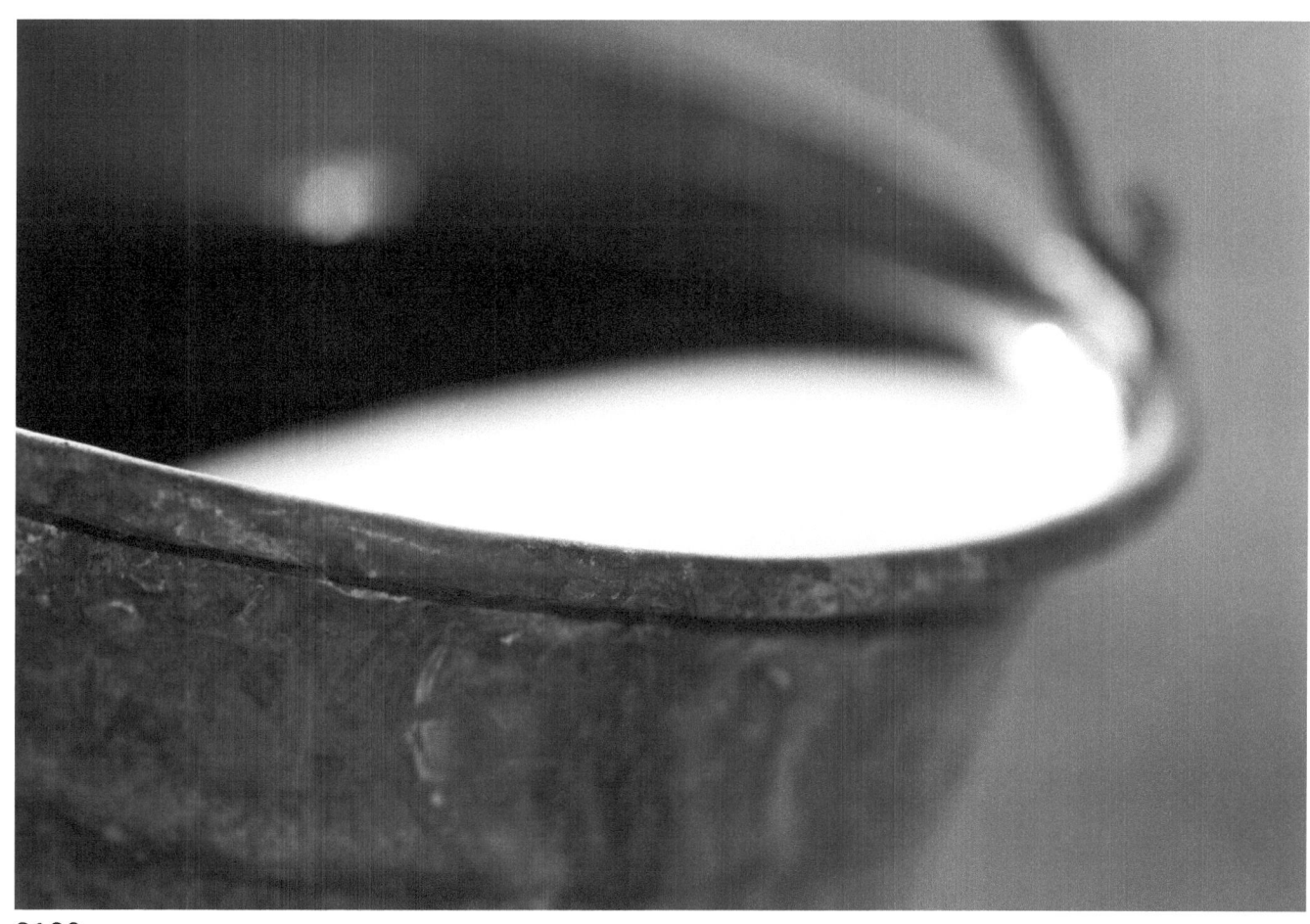

2180

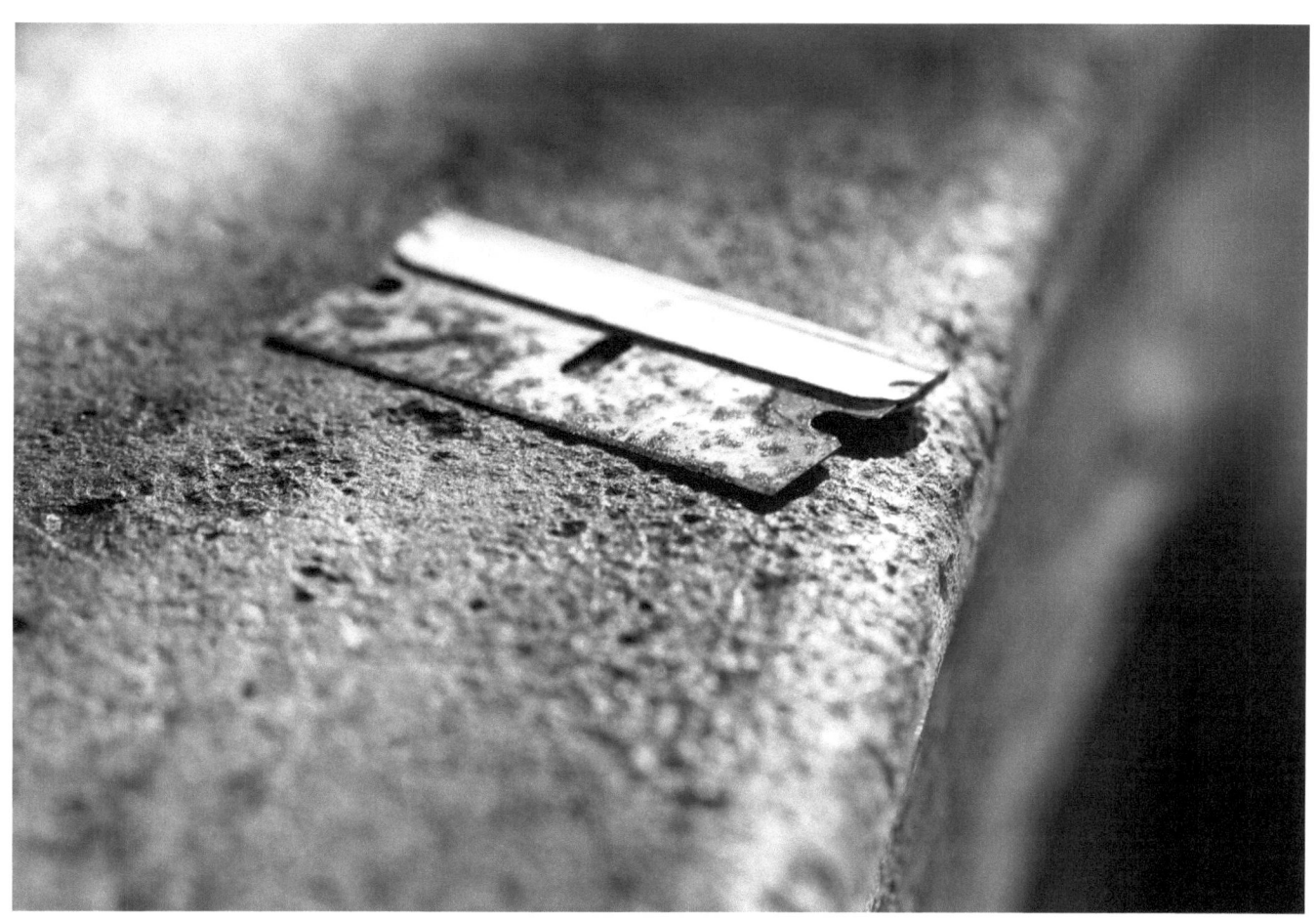

2467

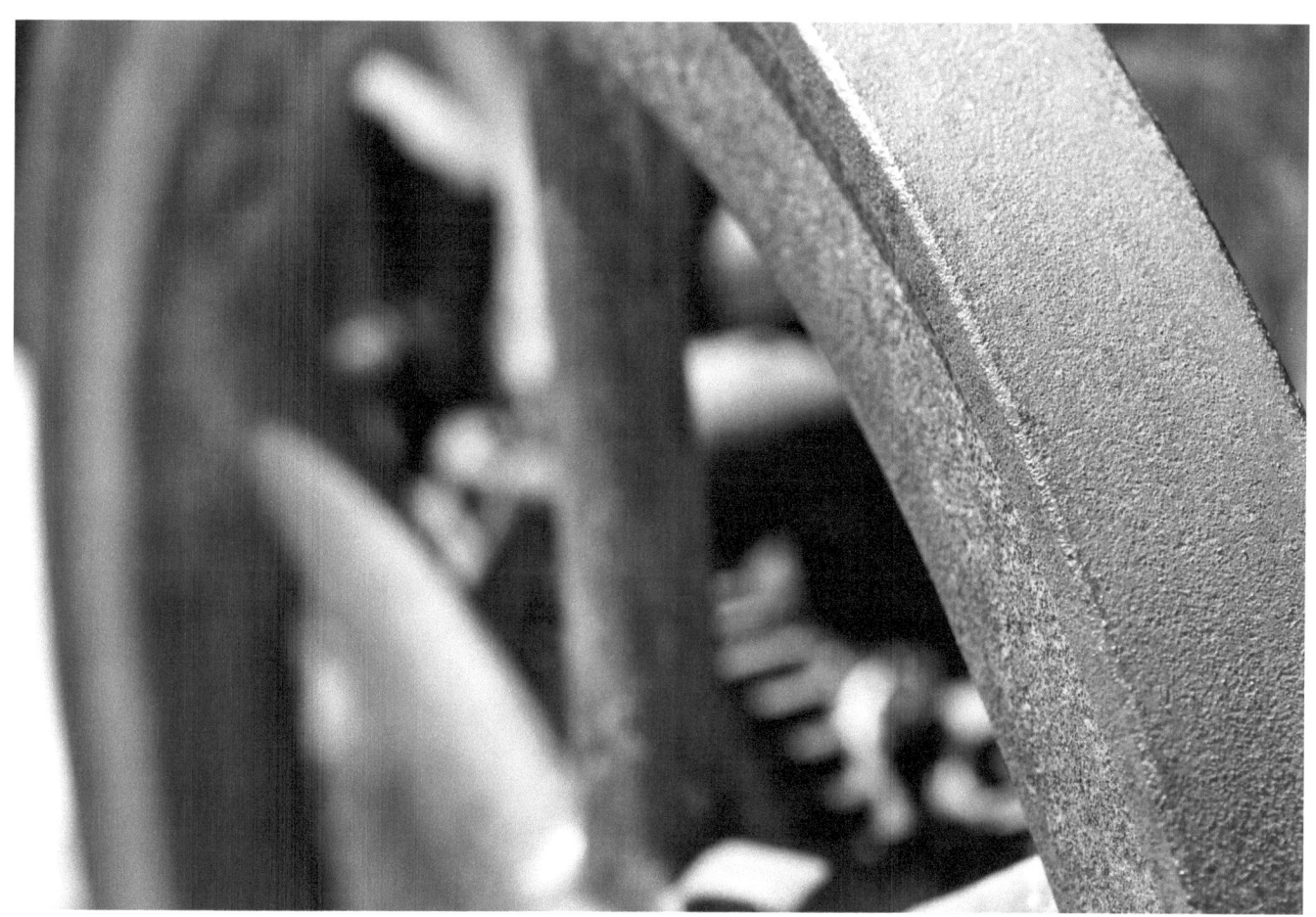

2962

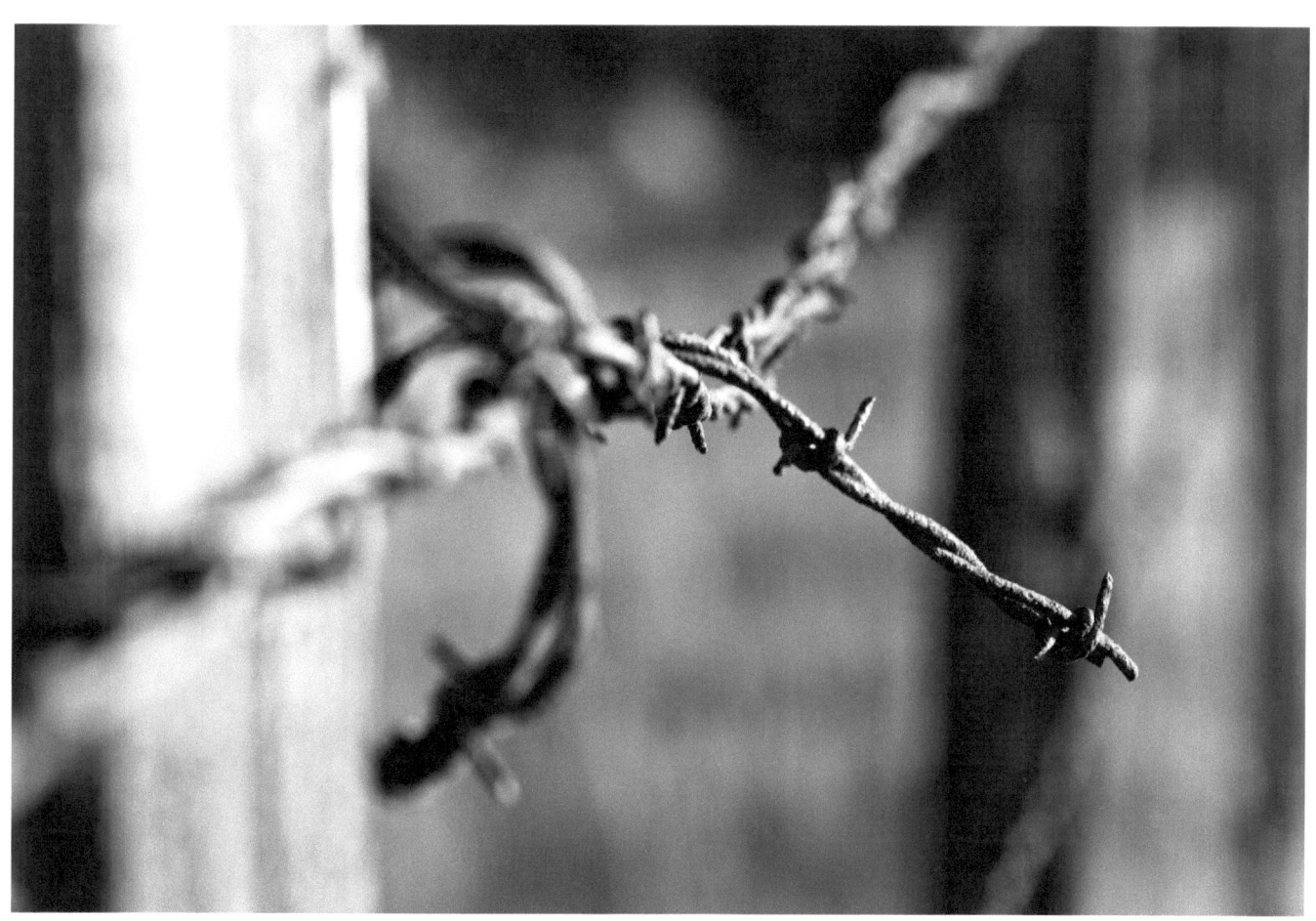

3359

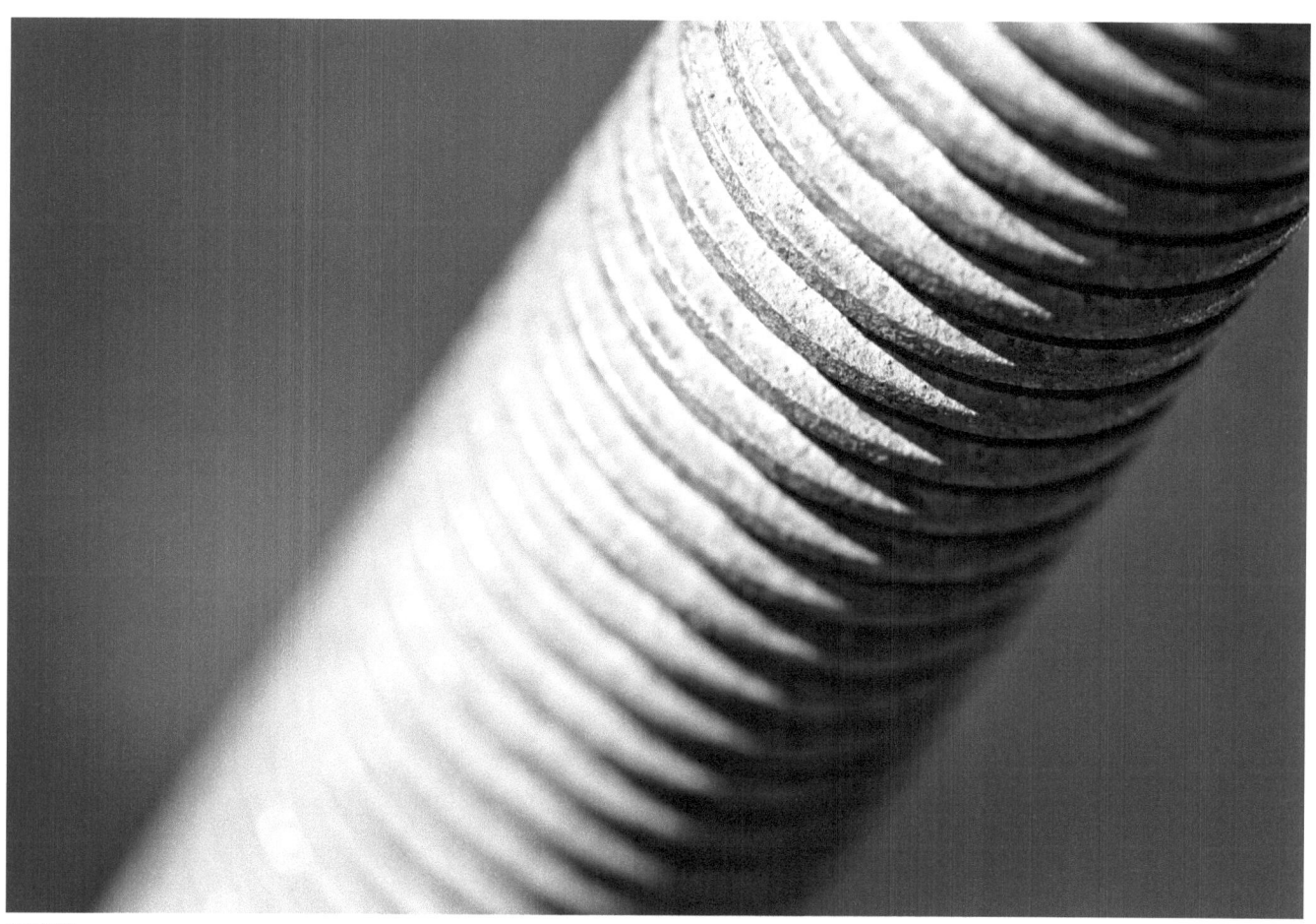

3937

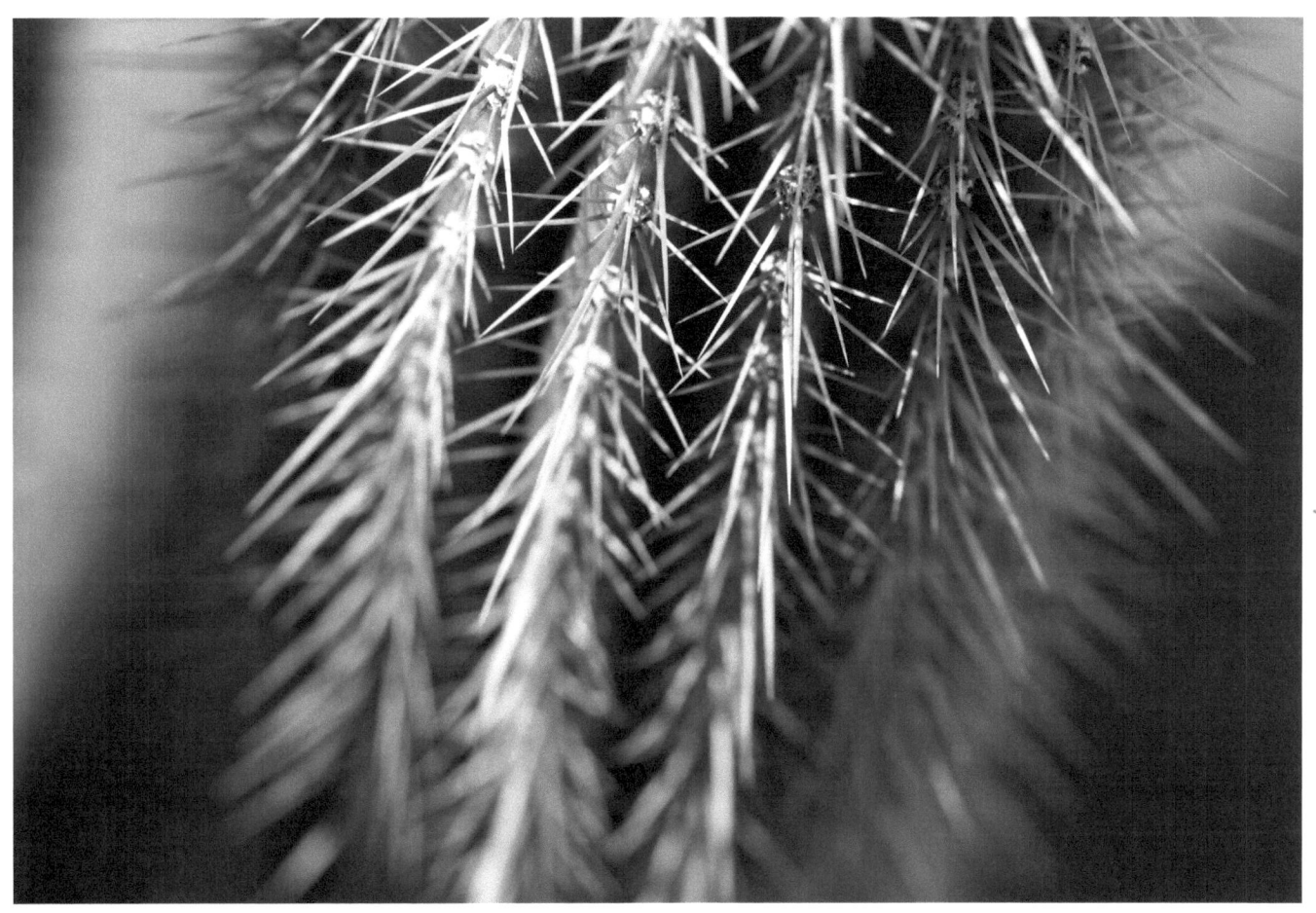

4070

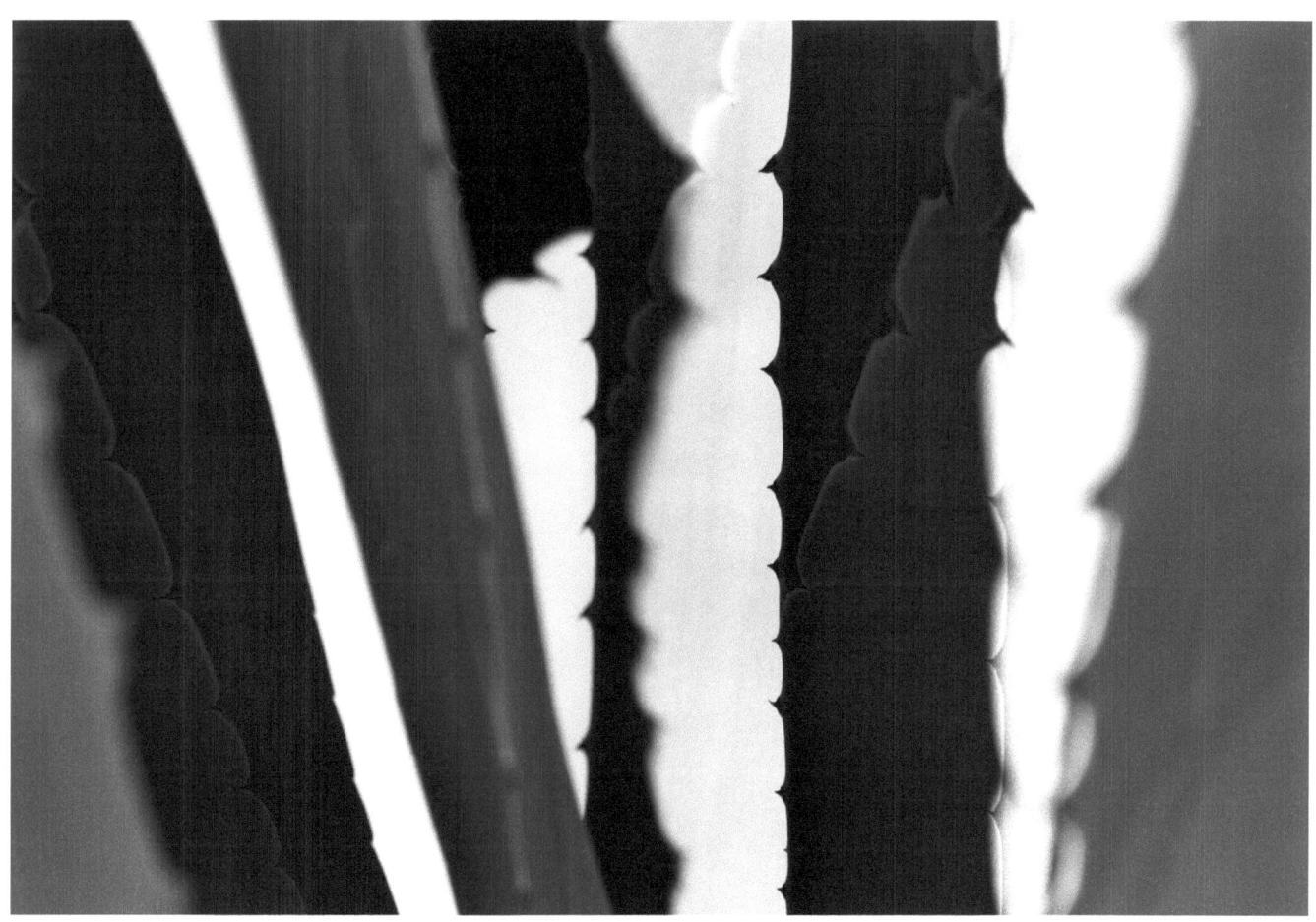

4099

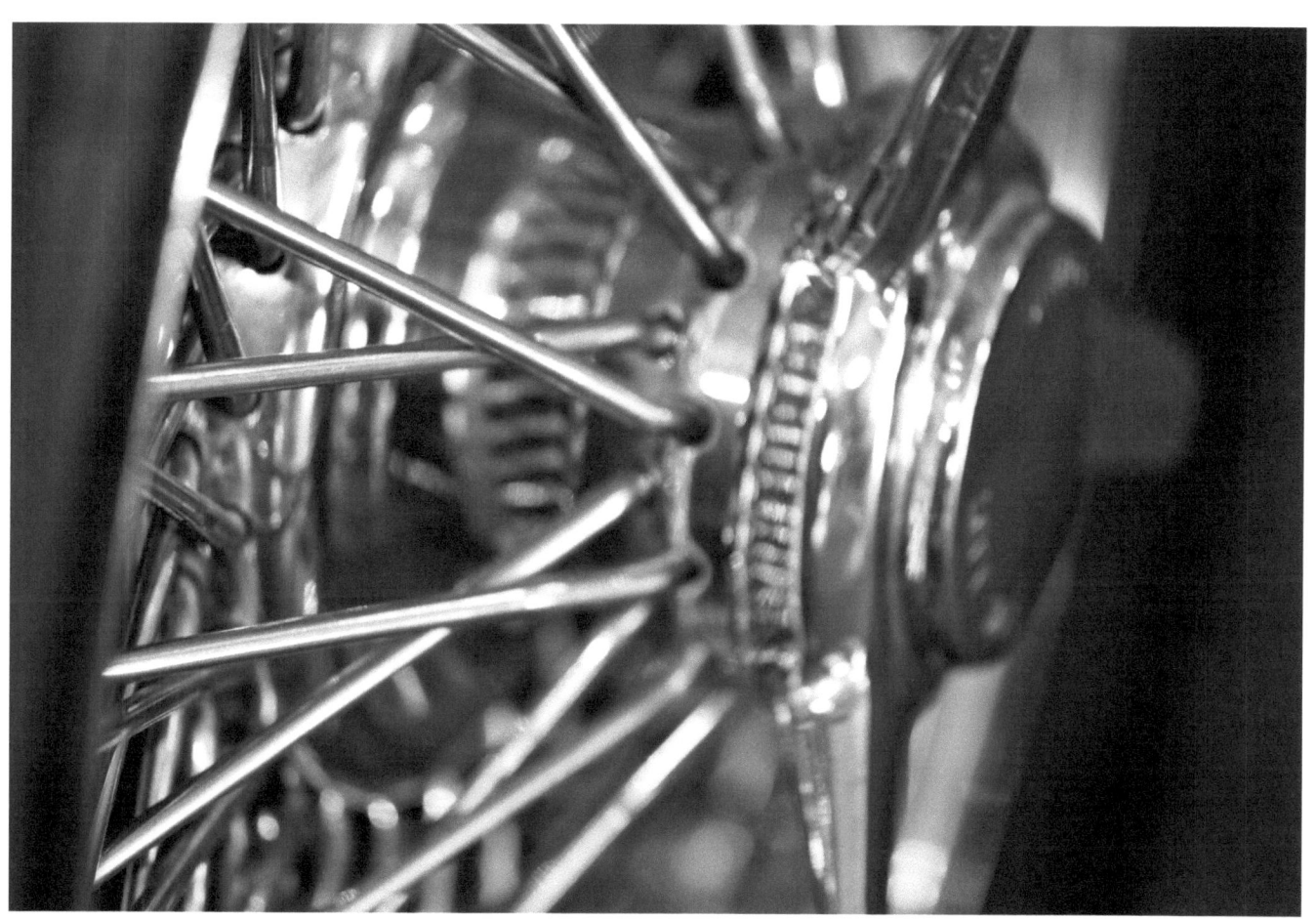

4193

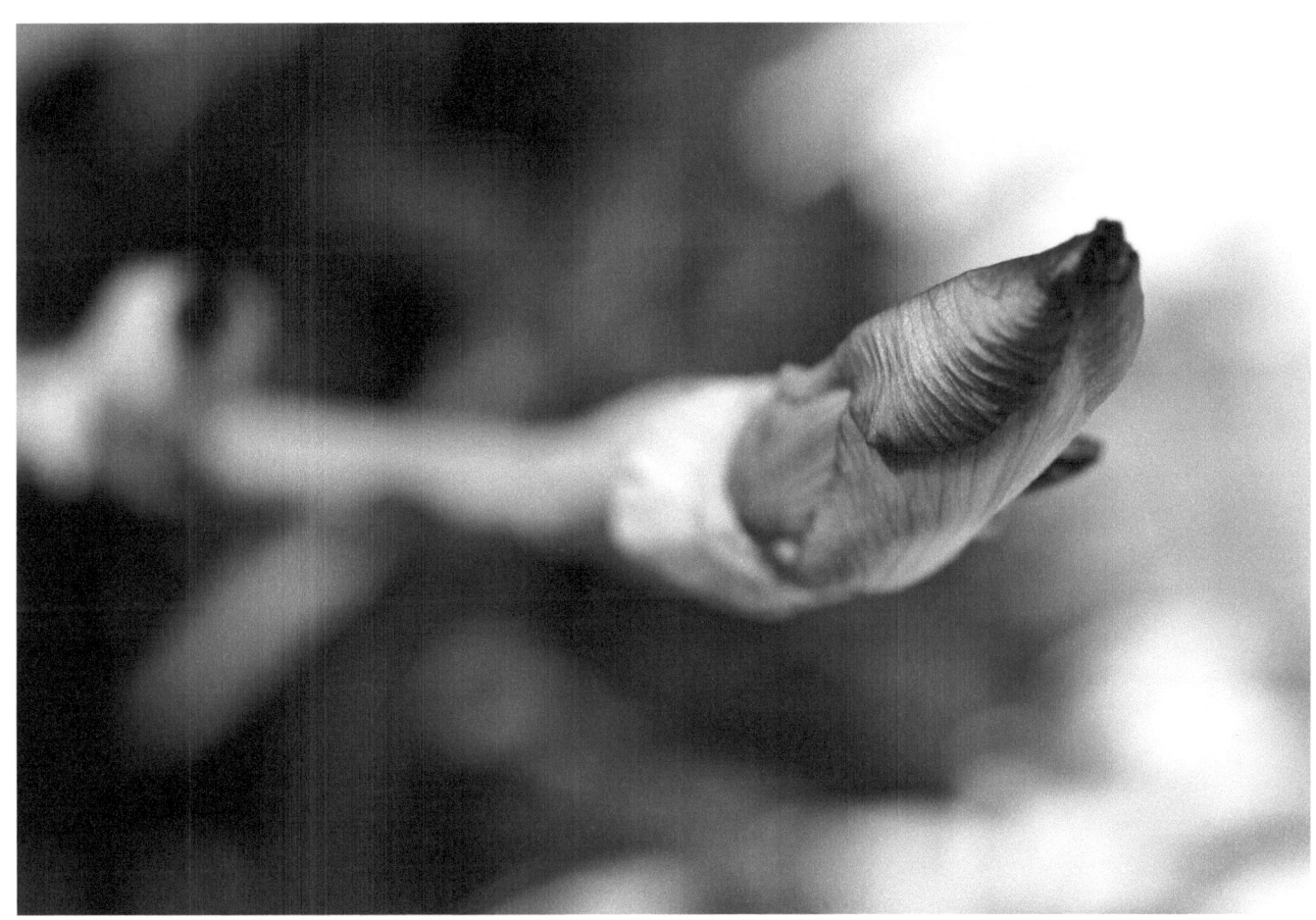

5492

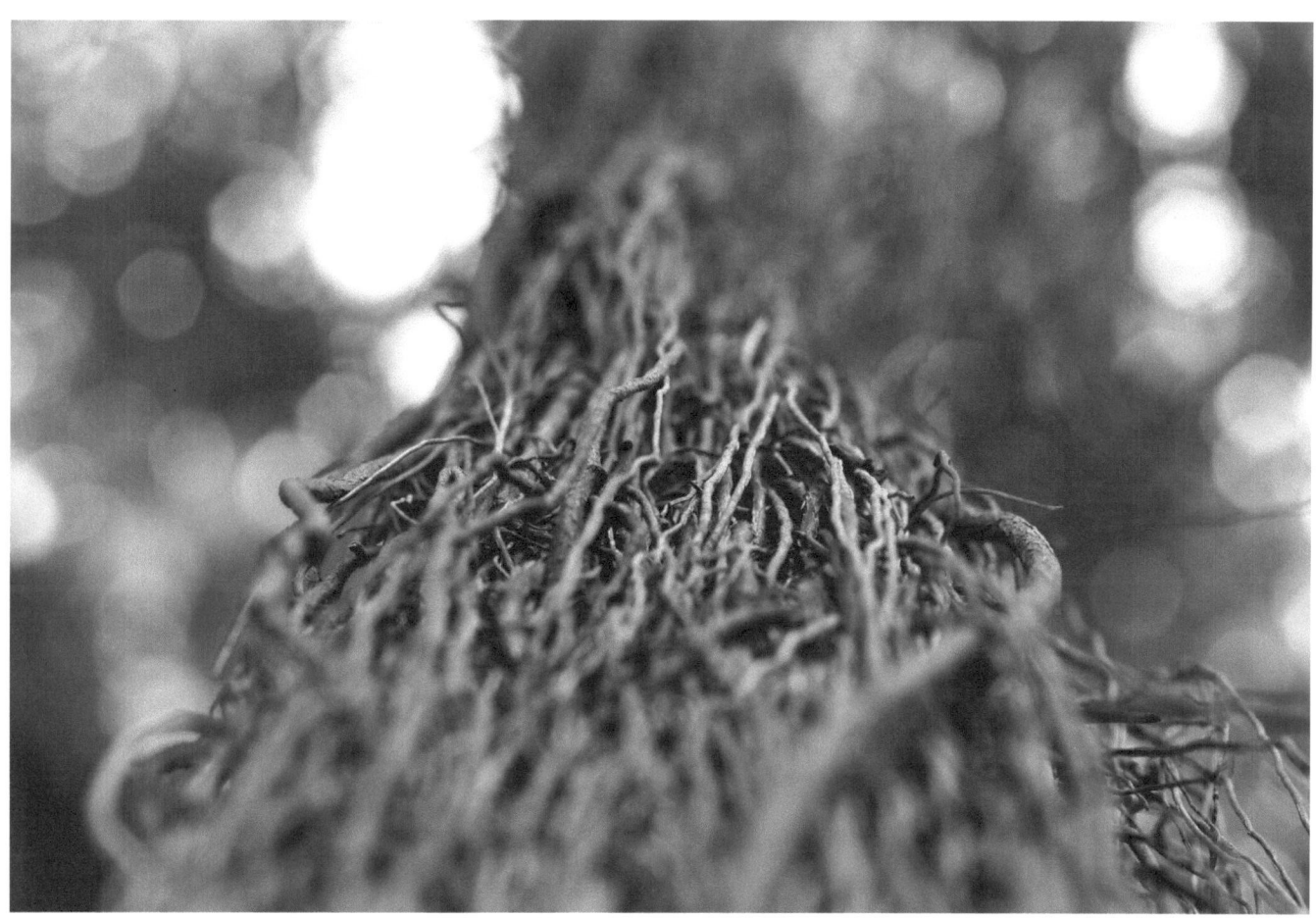

5811

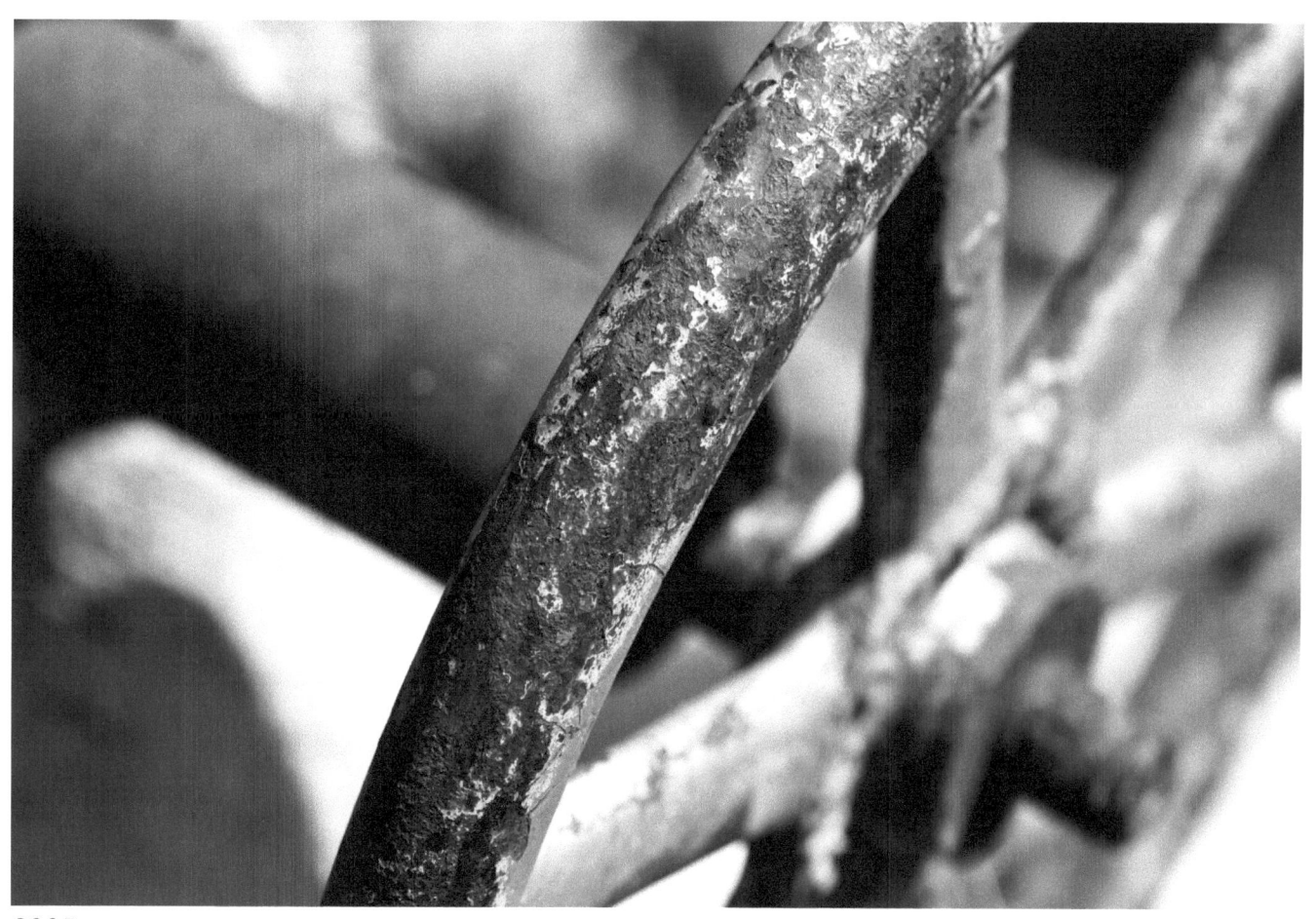

6095

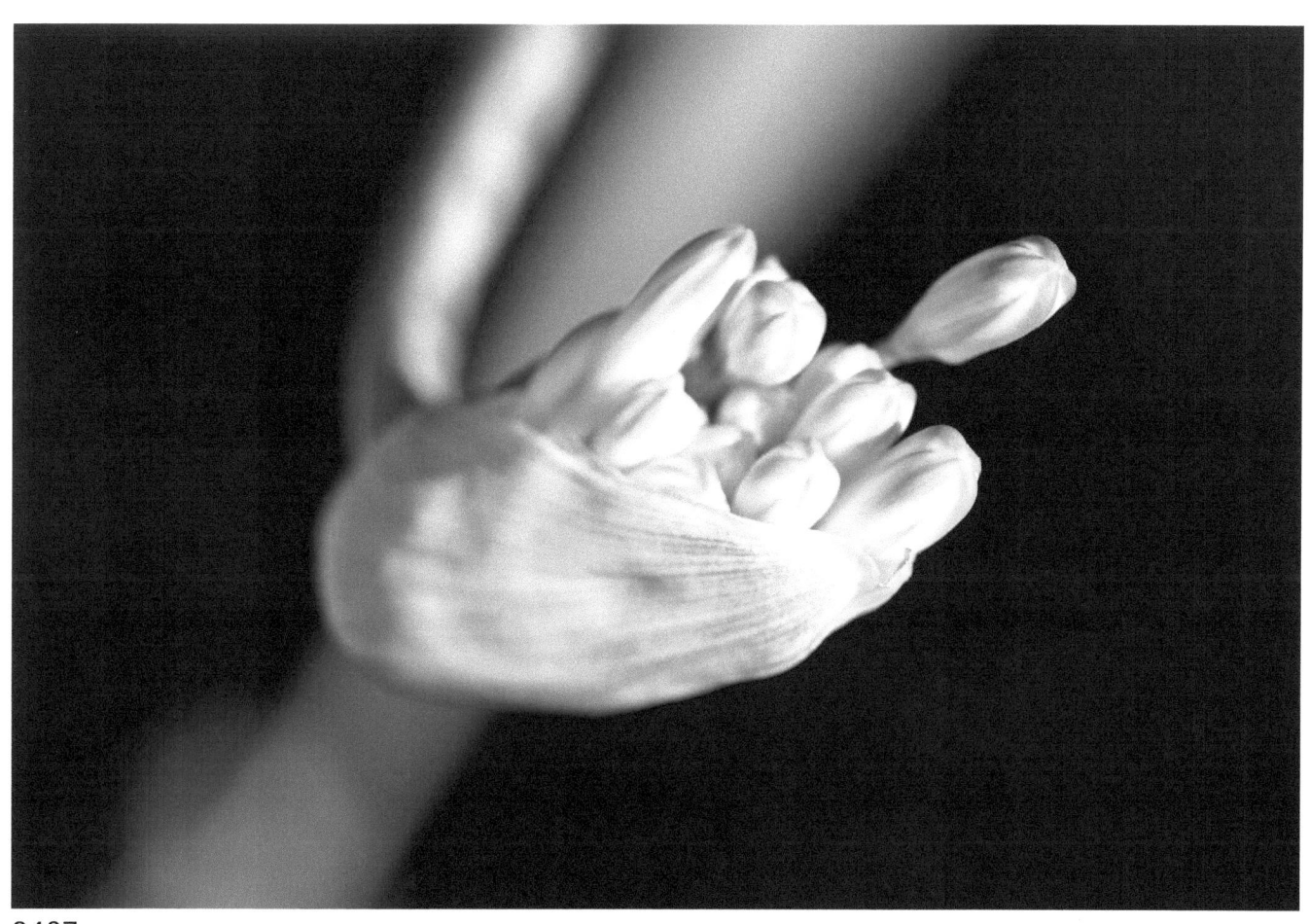

8407

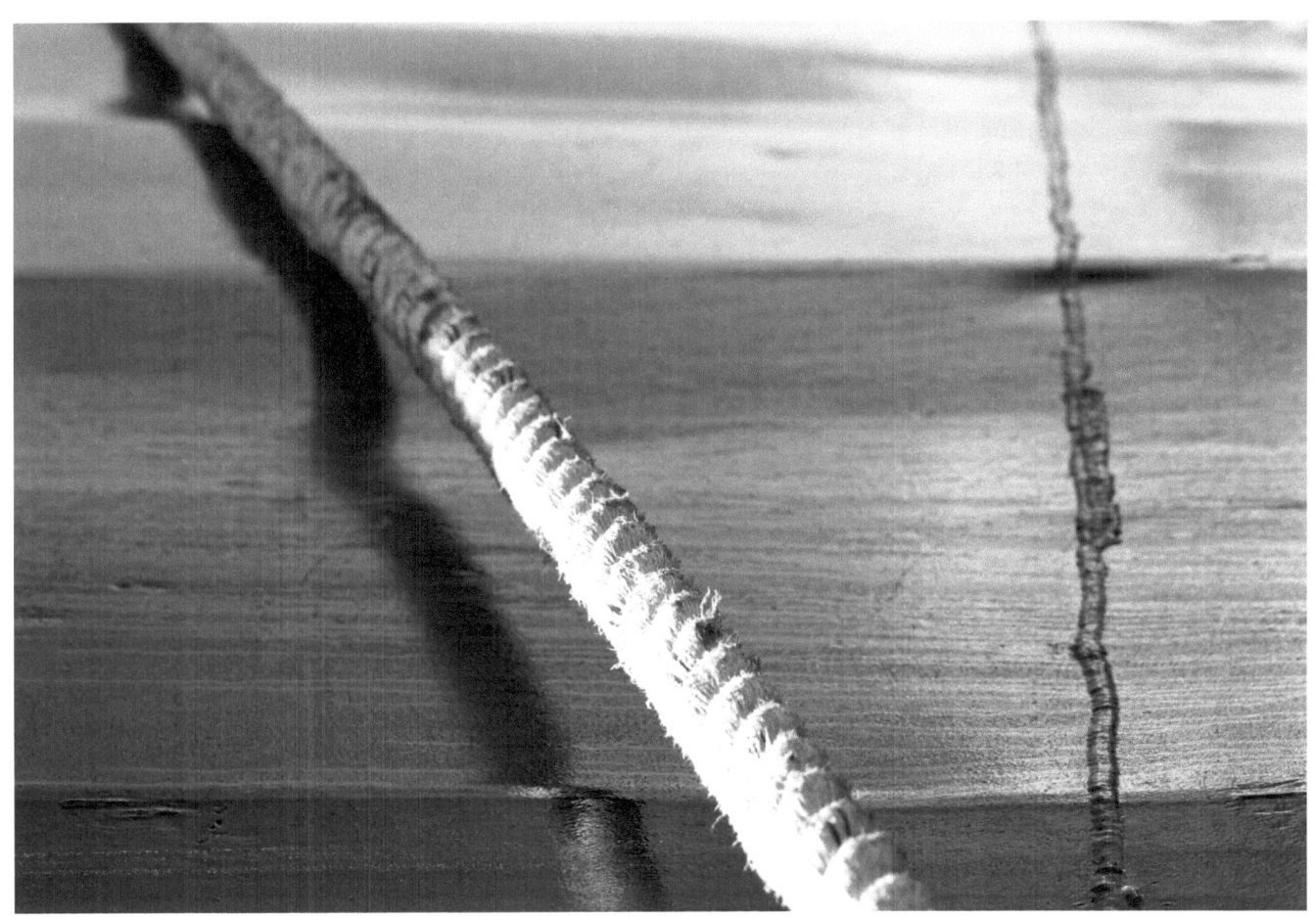

8470

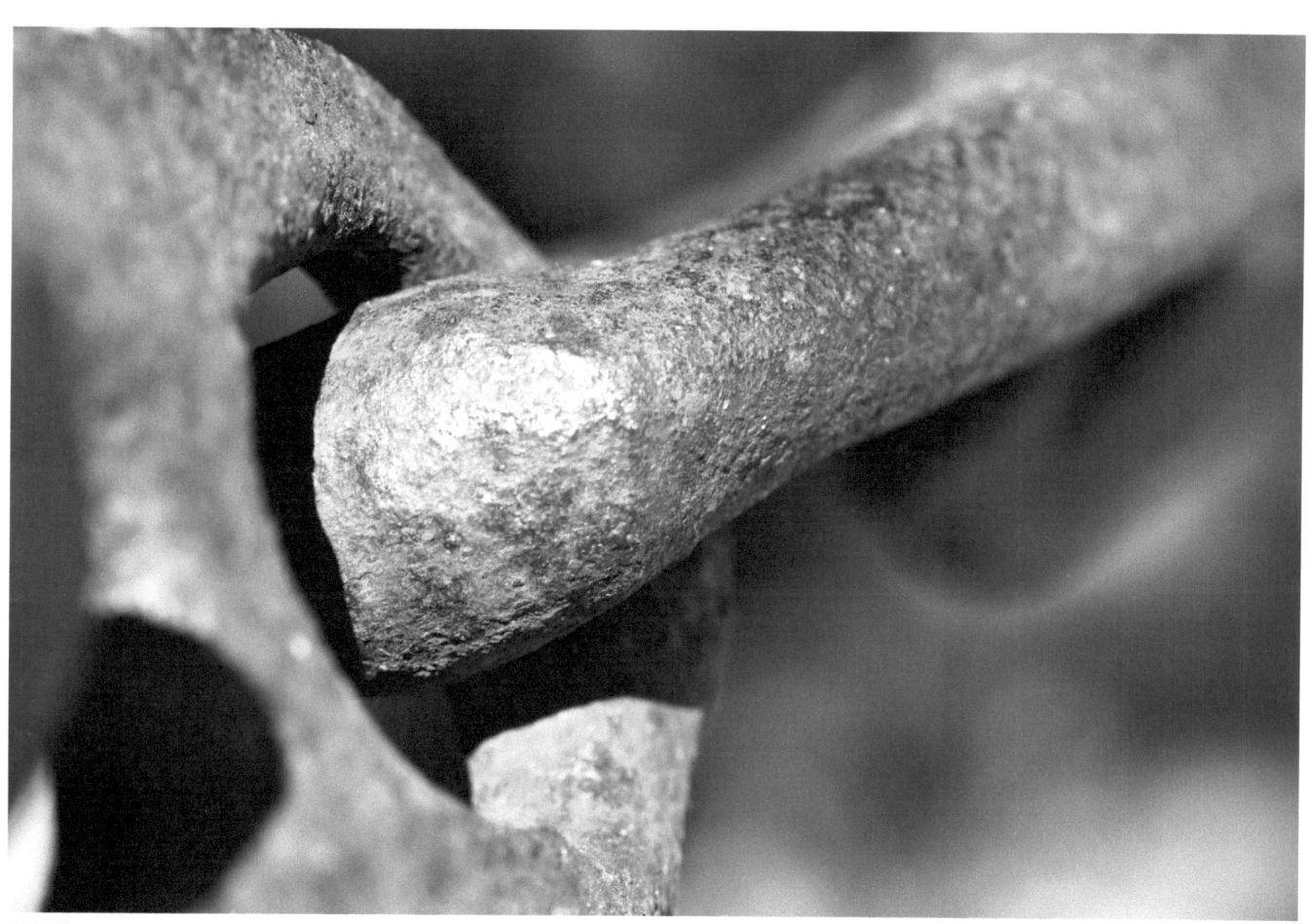

9353

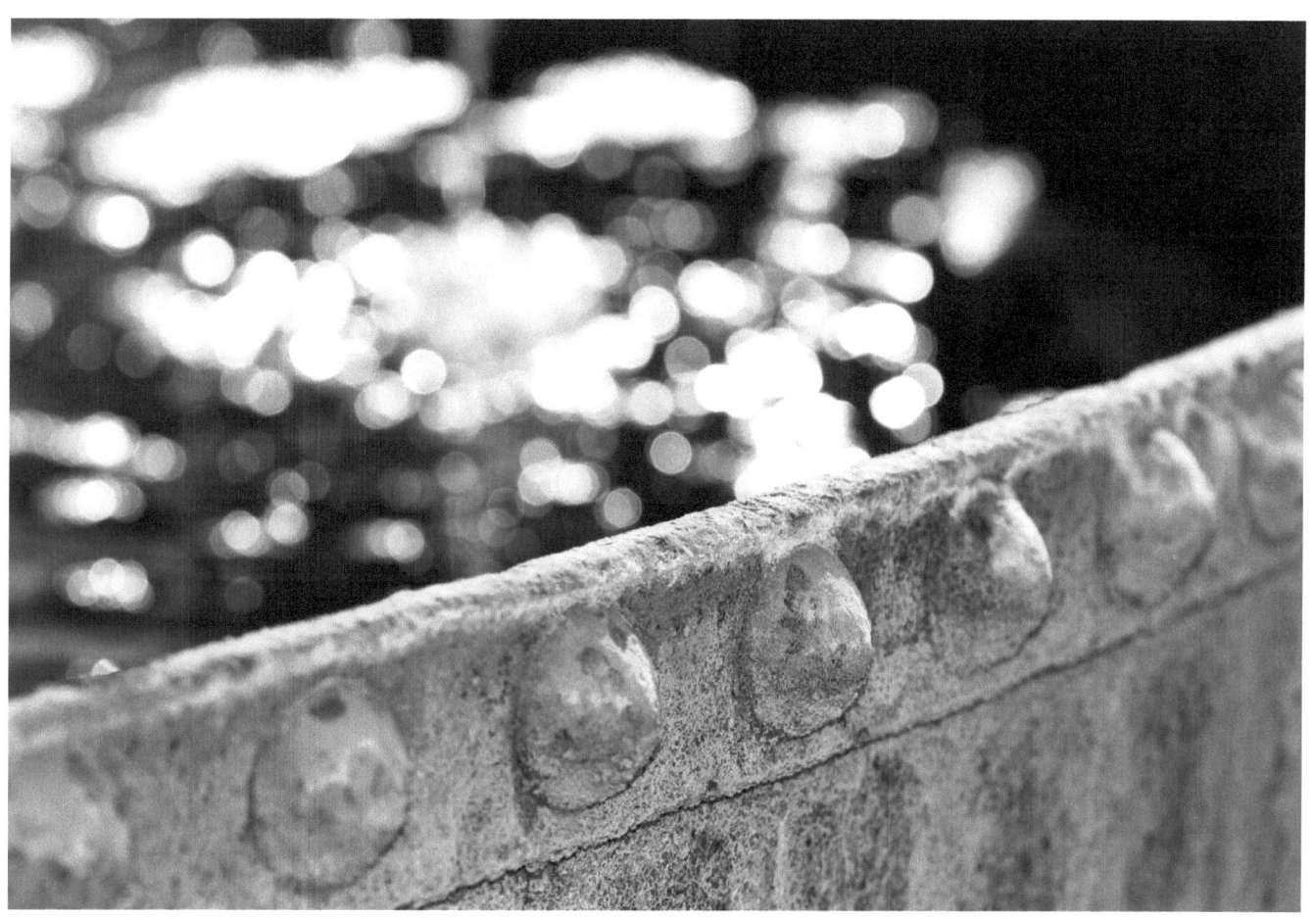

9430